The Profile Makers

A Marian Wood Book

Henry Holt and Company
New York

The Profile Makers

POEMS

Linda Bierds

Henry Holt and Company, Inc.
Publishers since 1866
115 West 18th Street
New York, New York 10011

Henry Holt® is a registered trademark
of Henry Holt and Company, Inc.

Published in Canada by Fitzhenry & Whiteside Ltd.,
195 Allstate Parkway, Markham, Ontario L3R 4T8.

Library of Congress Cataloging-in-Publication Data
Bierds, Linda.
The profile makers : poems / by Linda Bierds.—1st ed.
p.   cm.
"A Marian Wood book."
ISBN 0-8050-5535-5 (hardcover : alk. paper)
I. Title.
PS3562.I357P76   1997
811'.54—dc21   97-13623

Henry Holt books are available for special promotions and
premiums. For details contact: Director, Special Markets.

First Edition 1997

Designed by Kate Nichols

Printed in the United States of America
All first editions are printed on acid-free paper. ∞

1   3   5   7   9   10   8   6   4   2

For Frederick Kaplan

Grateful acknowledgment is made to the following publications, where these poems first appeared, some in a slightly different form: *The Atlantic Monthly:* "Safe," "The Weathervanes"; *Columbia: A Magazine of Verse:* "The Breaking-Aways," "Shawl: Dorothy Wordsworth at Eighty"; *Field:* "Altamira: What She Remembered," "The Suicide of Clover Adams: 1885," "Yellow Vision"; *The Journal:* "Edison: 1910," "Lawrence and Edison in New Jersey: 1923" "Vespertilio"; *The New Yorker:* "The Geographer," "The Three Trees"; *Parnassus: Poetry in Review:* "Muybridge"; *The Plum Review:* "From the Studio of Etienne de Silhouette: 1760"; *The Seattle Review:* "Burning the Fields"; *The Threepenny Review:* "Van Leeuwenhoek: 1675," "Balance".

I am grateful as well to the John Simon Guggenheim Memorial Foundation, the National Endowment for the Arts, and the Wolfers-O'Neill Foundation for their generous support.

My thanks to Beliz Brother, whose art installation, "Witness," inspired this book.

And always, to Marian Wood.

CONTENTS

This symbol is used to indicate a space between stanzas of a poem wherever such spaces are lost in pagination.

The Profile Makers

SIX IN ALL

PREFACE

Across the buckled, suck-hole roads,
my cousin, Mathew Brady's aide, bobbed
toward our scattered camp, his black-robed,
darkroom "whatsit wagon"—its pling
of glass plate negatives—half hearse, half cloaked
calliope. The Civil War was undeveloped
and camp was thick with families, the fields
a hail of scattered tents, their canvas cupping
counterpanes, quilts with hubs of rising suns.

He posed us near our tent's propped flap,
my parents shy against its wing, my toddler sister
tucked below, then waved us to a sudden freeze—
except for Jane, whose squirms became a handkerchief
or dove wing on the ether plate. He took
my father, stiff against the summer oaks,
then Mother's ragged silhouette—the two of them,
and us again, and Jane asleep. Six in all,
my family and chronicles of passing light,
the day by half-steps slipping down
across our heads and collarlines.

In later years, the war long cold, he found
in surplus its brittle song: long rooms
of glass plate negatives, with lesser ones,
he told me—snow-white carbines stacked in rows,

a soldier shoveling ghostly coal—
revived as greenhouse windows. *The houses
are magnificent, glass rows of smoky apparitions
that disappear, he said, when rains
begin, that melt, for human eyes at least, into
a kind of nothingness. Then only metal frames
are seen, like netting on the land.*

*I would find our family, he said, across
one building's southern wall,
where tandem trunks of windblown elms
arc toward hothouse limes . . .*

SIX IN ALL

ONE

From balsa's weightless wood, my father carved
the horse, then smoothed it to a foal,
then further still, into a kind of moon—horse yet,
and yet the head in soft relief was lunar, undefined—

as his is now, within the greenhouse wall. Erased
by my cousin's breath, perhaps, upon the plate, across
the damp collodion—his sigh or hum, some humanness
that hovers still, between my father's collarline
and globes of hothouse limes.

Two years beyond this negative, my father drowned
off Georgia's shore—so twice was slain by breathing.
They say on death the lungs accept the sea, inhale
its foreign element, the way I think the shutter's mouth
draws time inside to timelessness.

Before he died, he wrote that flocks of braying mares
were dropped by sling from battleships to waiting scows,
their stiffened legs like walking canes,
the flashing cane-tips of their hooves.

"For those of us on wet-decked scows, a dozen times
they broke the sun, a dozen dust-caked underbreasts
cast their quick eclipse . . ."

And did I recall our balsa foal? From rye and fern,
from loops of waxy thread, how we wove her green arena?
"God, to have that footing now!—turf instead of
sickly sea, that swings me like some sling-strung beast."

Within the glass plate negative, he waits
near summer oaks: coat sharp, shirt sharp, but face
dissolved to clouds. Across the plate's transparent sky,
the hothouse air has spawned an emerald scum,
a silken vegetation that spreads
its spidered reach. He stands below, coat sharp,
shirt sharp, his head dissolved to clouds.
It will support him soon, the green.

From the Studio of
Etienne de Silhouette: 1760

"Ice is the sire of water,
and yellow the sire of green . . ."

In the darkened room the child listens,
feet propped on the chair rungs
and the marshflower scent of the lard lamp
so heavy around her. She sits between
its steady light and a leaf of vellum
tacked to the attic wall, while the other,
Silhouette, kneels and traces her pigeon profile.

". . . and before the green there is yellow,
and before the yellow
ice slumps through the dark champaign . . ."

Now he is cutting two families of paper—
vellum and coal—guiding the scissors
down the trace line.

". . . and the hoofed beasts, clicking over the ice field,
bleat to each other in the half-light.
And the bleats skate away, become
shorter, shorter, until they are . . . what?
Just the skipped stones of a bird's chirrup.
Then the yellow begins . . ."

He has pulled back the curtains to midday,
its landscape of steeples, horse carts. She blinks,
dips to her fixed likeness:
blunt brow, collar, two blisters of button.

". . . at times in the midst of their roaming,
the beasts fold down to the ice, stretch over its fabric
and sleep. And the heat from their still bodies
melts a beast-shaped pool beneath them.
They awake to take water from their glistening profiles—
quickly, of course, before ice re-closes, before

hoof and haunch sink back into nothing.
Lovely, I think, on that wide champaign,
each furred beast sipping from its likeness—
lying down at times, I am certain,
just to rise up and drink."

The Three Trees

Late day. A wash of claret at the window.
And the room swells with the odor of quince,
tin-sharp and dank, as the acid creeps down
through the etch marks. He dips the foreground languidly,
Rembrandt, so thickets will darken, the horse
and lovers resting there, the bamboo latitude
of fishing pole, the shadowed river.

Then inks it all—mixed sky, three dappled trees—
and presses the intricate net of it
to the white-bleached etching sheet below: one skein
of storm aligning the nothingness, one haycart
rich with villagers. At the window now,

a fading to ochre. And beyond,
through the streets and valley, at the base
of a hillock thick with three trees, a hunter
is ringing a treble bell, its quick bite
driving the field birds to the sheltering grasses.
Around him, dark in their earth-colored clothes,
others are throwing a slack-weave net

out over the meadow and scuttering birds.
And up from their various hands, quick fires bloom,
rush through the beard grass, the birds bursting up

to the capturing net, some dying of fright,
some of flames, some snuffed by the hunters

like candles. A breeze begins, slips through the tree limbs.
Slung over each hunter are threadings of birds,
strung through the underbeak. Pleat-works of plenitude,
down the back, the curve of the shoulder.
They offer their warmth in slender lines,
as sunlight might, through the mismatched shutters
of a great room, the long gaps casting

their cross-hatch. As if time itself might spin them all
down some vast, irreversible pathway—
haycart, hunter, small bowl with its blossoms of quince—
and the simple patterns resting there
barred everything back from the spinning.

The Geographer

From the painting by Vermeer

There. Out the window. They are burning the flood fields.
And the light that touches his forehead
is softened by smoke. He is stopped in a long robe,
blue with a facing of pumpkin. In his hand,
the splayed legs of a compass taper to pin tips.

It is noon. Just after dawn, he took
for his errant heart a paper of powdered rhubarb
and stoops to the window now, half in pain, half
in love with the hissing fields:

mile after mile of cane stalks, fattened
with drawn water. Such a deft pirouette, he thinks,
flood pulled up through the bodies of cane, then
water cane burned into steam, and steam like mist
on the fresh fields, sucked dry for the spring planting.

Powdered rhubarb. Like talc on the tongue.
And what of this heart, this blood? Harvey writes
that the washes of pulse do not ebb, do not
flow like the sea, but circle, draw up to the plump heart.
And is that the centering spirit then? Red plum,
red shuffling mole . . . ?

When the flood waters crested, dark coffins
bobbed down through the cane stalks like blunt pirogues.

And then in the drift, one slipper
and the ferreting snouts of radishes.

He touches his sleeve, looks down to his small desk,
pale in its blanket of map, all the hillsides
and carriageways, all the sunken stone walls
reduced to the sweep of a pin tip.
They are burning the flood fields—such a hissing, hissing,

like a landscape of toads. And is that how blood
circles back in its journey, like water through
the body of the world? And the great, flapping fire, then—
opening, withering—in its single posture
both swelling and fading—is that the human heart?

Van Leeuwenhoek: 1675

All day, the cooper's hoops squeal and nibble.
Through the single eyepiece of his hand-ground lens,
he watches a spider's spinnerets, then the tail-strokes
of spermatozoa. Now and then, his bald eye unsquints,
skates blindly across his wrist and sleeve—
and makes from his worlds their reversals:
that of the visible and that of the seen . . .

Visible? he is asked, at the market, or the stone tables
by the river. The lip of the cochineal? Starch
on the membranes of rice? But of course—
though a fashioned glass must press and circle,
tap down, tap down, until that which is, is.

Until that which is, breaks to the eye.
It is much like the purslane, he tells them,
that burst from the hoofbeats of horse soldiers:
black seeds long trapped in their casings, until
the galloping cracked them. In the steppes, he says,

or veldt, where nothing in decades had traveled.
Then flowers burst forth from the trauma
of hoof-taps, and left in the wake of the soldiers
a ribbon of roadway as wide as their riding.

Smoke now. The screech of a shrinking hoop.
His thoughts are floral with hearth flames and soldiers,
the cords in his bent neck rigid as willow.
Then slowly, below, something yellow begins. Some flutter of
yellow on the glass plate, in the chamber of a tubal heart . . .

By winter, the snows crossed over the flanks
of the horses, felling them slowly. And the soldiers,
retreating, so close to survival, crept
into the flaccid bellies. Two nights,
or three, hillocks of entrails steaming like
breath. Now and then they called out
to each other, their spines at the spines
of the long horses, and the flaps of muscle
thick shawls around them. Then they rose, as a thaw
cut a path to the living.

. . . A flutter, yellow, where an insect heart ripples
in reflex. But no, it is only light and shadow, light
turning shadow. As the perfect doors, in their terrible
finitude, open and open.

He straightens, feels his body swell
to the known room. Such vertical journeys, he thinks,
down, then back through the magnifications

of light. And the soldiers, their cloaks
like blossoms on a backdrop of snow:
surely, having taken through those hours
both the cradle and the grave,
they could enter any arms and sleep.

The Diagnostic Silhouettes of
John Lavater: 1795

They speak.
No sway of the eye, no turn
of the lip, no gesture, twitch,
but still, the line of their language
circles the listening ear. As here, the
angle of this forehead sings a clear and
brilliant fancy. And the too round lips?
Good cheer! With a verge to inoffensive
cunning. And these, the slant of nose, the
crest of chin: quick violence balanced with
discretion. By lamplight freeze a crowd upon
a wall, and there, through cap flap or countenance,
the timid, sanguine, genial, maidenly gather, in pairs
or singly, their darkened postures florid with intent,
with loss, with mastery, with the slopes of all past
and possible passions. Mute shadows, you say.
Crisp ghosts. But I will trust the talents
of the firmer parts, bone and gristle,
the nature of the flesh they frame. I
will trust the oblique nose, the single
brow, the arc that curves from birth to
grave, the echoes etched in soil. More
than the mutable muscle's pull, more
than the kiss or whisper,
I will trust—like letters
bound in looping script—the
language of the grand outline.

SIX IN ALL

TWO

"*Now hold,*" *he said, his bloated words*
afloat in the black-cloaked chamber.
And Mother stopped in profile. She had turned
to witness lifting moths, their thrum
across the oaks, then held to watch that tuft of air

that was the moths, empty yet filled
with tracks of the missing, like
the crease her cast-off headscarf left,
crown to milky ear. I stood outside the camera's frame,

near tables fat with yellowed shirts and vats
of crystal vinegar. Beyond the oaks, a soldier
worked against a plow, leaned back across
its harness straps, as if to cancel cultivation,
as if to close the trough that foamed before him.
His uniform was stiffened wool, his shirt fresh blue
against the field: half farmer still, half infantry,
a slanted shape that branched between
two worlds of burial.

My mother swallowed, saw the shutter spiral down,
her face a blend of dust and wonder—
that she might gather over glass, that she might claim,
across the flecks of bromide salt, some bygone self.

The sunlight cast quick glints against the plow,
across the rippling skins of vinegar.
My mother laughed, stepped forward

through the grass. Once she penned a note in vinegar's ink—
invisible, but for blisters wetness leaves. Like magic,
she said, how heat will mark each letter's path. Some greeting,

I think, her words so short-lived their birth
was withdrawal. We held the page to a candle's flame
and letters stroked up on mottled wings.
Then "Look," she whispered, "their quickening shapes:
the thumb-plump, the sickled,
the branching-away . . ."

Shawl: Dorothy Wordsworth at Eighty

Any strong emotion tempers my madnesses.
The death of beloveds. William in his fever-coat.
I reenter the world through a shallow door
and linger within it, conversations returning,
the lateral cycle of days.

I do not know what it is that removes me,
or sets me again at our long table, two crescents
of pike on a dark plate. But memory lives then,
and clarity. Near my back once again,
our room with a brook at the baseworks,
its stasis of butter and cheese. Or there,

in a corner, my shawl of wayside flowers.
Orchis and chickory. Little tongues of birth-wort.

I remember a cluster of autumn pike
and a dark angler on the slope of the weir.
The fish in his hand and the roiling water
brought forth with their brightness
his leggings and waist. But his torso was lost
into shadow, and only his pipe smoke survived,
lifting, then doubling, on the placid water above him.

Often, I think, I encompass a similar shadow.

But rise through it, as our looped initials
once rose over dye-stained eggs.
We were children. With the milk of a burning candle
we stroked our letters to the hollowed shells.
And dipped them, then, in a blackberry bath,
until the script of us surfaced,
pale, independent, the *D* and cantering *W.*

Then *C* for Christopher. *V*—William laughed—for vale.
And *P,* he said, for Pisces, Polaris, the gimballing
planets. And for plenitude, perhaps,
each season, each voice in its furrow of air . . .

Once, I was told of a sharp-shinned hawk
who pursued the reflection of its fleeing prey
through three striations of greenhouse glass:
the arrow of its body cracking first into anteroom,
then desert, then the thick mist
of the fuchsias. It lay in a bloodshawl
of ruby flowers, while the petals of glass
on the brick-work floor repeated its image.
Again and again and again.
As all we have passed through sustains us.

Altamira: What She Remembered

That, chased by a covey of hunters, the fox
slipped into its den
exactly as bread slipped into her father's mouth:
white with a tapering backstroke of brown.

That the hunters at the den door
chopped and chopped with their black heels.

That the cave they revealed, child-sized but
humid with promise, ticked
with a placid rain, as if the weather
of the sky were the weather of the earth.

That she saw on the cave walls, in blue-black
and ochre, "the bulls," although they were bison,
she learned, and a dipping hind.

That the borders of her body were the borders
of the weather.

That whatever awakened within her there—
not grief, not fear—had the sound
of hooves down a cobbled street.

That they lifted her back by one arm.

formatting ornament
∽

That, as she walked with her father
through the downland, the sound of the hooves
settled.

That whatever awakened within her there
had the sound of birds
flushed from the downland grasses.

Had the sound of leaves from a pitchfork's tines.

Years later, had the ticking sound of the rain.

Balance

L. J. M. Daguerre

There were red-pocked duck eggs deep in the quince.
And walks to the chemist.
It was summer, before mercury vapors
and pale amalgams, before time balanced
on a silvered plate, perpetually present,

perpetually past. I remember jugglers
in the wide cafés. And tumblers. The jester's bells
thick on their cap flaps.
I danced, then conquered the tightrope

in the style of the great Furioso!
Slack and tufted, it hung between
porches of primrose and the spidering shells
of a yellow ivy.
          My pant legs tied, my slippers
so soft the toe knuckles surfaced—
like the snouts of carp on a still pond—
and the flagstones below,
and the circular tables, their lacquered reflections
of forearms and chins. Then the sawstrokes
of rope on the plantar arch—as if

ᒡ

to divide my impossible cargo,
my flap-armed, grounded, airborne body,
both dipping and risen, both this side and that.

Someone sneezed—always—
                and toppled me,

my knuckles and knee joints breaking the fall.

I would hang inverted as Yesterday—just over
the present, just under the past—
with the flagstones at my back a kind of sky,
and above me, which was now below,
the balcony bottoms. And farther, below, where
the late sky offered its fresh earth,
the rooflines and eaves,
all the doves in their darkening chambers.

Yellow Vision

She is each of their unaware subjects,
slumped in the corner of some night café,
her face, hair, the velvet choker at her throat,
all cast in a yellowing
limelight. It is France, the close
of the nineteenth century. Painters
and haystacks. And the wormwood toxin
that poisons her vision, magnifies theirs,
each brain temporarily stained
by a terpene sheen. Xanthopsia, it is called—
yellow vision—too much absinthe, thick
in its fluted cup, and the world, the palette
and proprietor's apron, the lakes and cypresses:
yellow, golden, apple green.

She is subject. They are painters, sipping
absinthe, until canvas after canvas
gilds to a sickly chill. All the wheat fields,
all the lank burlesque, oddly slanted, raw.
And now she is walking down the fallow roadway.
In the opening light, steam
slides from the cows and rooftops, from
the wormwood blossoms pale on the hillside.
Her room smells of milk, then an oiled wool. And why
would they lend to the harvests and dance halls

෧—

this gloss of misgiving? Why would they court
these distortions of light, cup after cup, until
the hue-thickened visible spectrum
shrivels to yellow?
On the table her daughter's wooden doll
rests in a mane of cornsilk hair, the strands
withered dark and matted. Soon she will draw
from a thick husk a handful of silk, then re-pin
new hair for the fresh day. Brilliant,
it will cling to her skin like the opening hour,
though she flicks her hands, shaking
the slender strands. Still some will cling,
earth-cool and brilliant. And will not
take their moment from her
for all of her shaking.

Vespertilio

Julia Margaret Cameron

Like winter fog, the coal dust climbs her stockings,
although the coal itself has long departed, tumbled
barrow by barrow to an alternate shelter.
She scrubs the floor, sets across the gaping boards
square vats of rank collodion, of alcohol
and pyrogallol. Still the coal dust blooms,
until her apron darkens and her hem-strokes
brush to the path's pale stones

a soft hieroglyphics. She has walked
to the glass henhouse and bundles the hens
to their new roost, one wing at her breast, one wing
in her hand, the stiff legs riding her forearm.
Their livingness, she says, touching
a wattle and ruby comb, the tepid feet that stretch,
then curl, like something from the sea.

So the coalshed becomes her darkroom
and the henhouse welcomes the bent Carlyle,
Darwin and Tennyson, Browning, Longfellow,
each posed near a curtained backdrop, each
sharp in his livingness: a glaze of amber earwax,
a leaf of tobacco like ash on the beard.
But the portraits . . . Unfocused, critics say. The lens

stepping down into fog. Aberrant. Distorted. Although
she prefers Undefined, as in Not yet captured

by the language of this world. They are rich
with the inner, she answers, with a glimpse of the soul
flapping up through collodion baths,

darkly transparent, like the great bats
that flap near the henhouse windows. She watches them
break at dusk past the tree line
then flash at the windows and flash, as if
they are seeking their lost counterparts—although
they are not birds, of course, but dense with wings,
so dense the sleek, half-opened wings

would cover a wattle, a comb, and opening, easily
cover the back, the breast,
and easily opening cover the tail,
the yellow, tepid, stretching feet: as
a dark sea spreads over its garden.

SIX IN ALL

THREE

That we could block these warring worlds—the native
from the fashioned—would make my mother flinch,
although she dips against an oak with languid
resolution, Jane in fever at her feet, my father
with his pipe bowl lifted, pinched,
as he might gently pinch
some brier sparrow into flight . . . that
on this greenhouse wall our faded wisps of family,
reversed to smoky filaments, could keep
the cool and hot apart . . .

At times when stark daylight recedes, my present face
in pale reflection, bobs
near its childhood other—while under the dappled
layers of us, slack-jawed orchids steam.

Two worlds. Or one, perhaps. Two rival
atmospheres. Once my father crept beneath the sea,
along some vein of miner's shaft. He told
how shaft heat sucked and swelled,
how pallid torsos of the men
gleamed like pulpit lilies. The icy sea so close above
a pin might bring it down, he said.
Two dozen fathoms rushing by. Just overhead,

he heard the boulders shift and roll,
like great-boots pacing on his grave . . .

He tossed the brier bird—launched it into flame,
at least—then stepped into the war. Can you believe,
he wrote to us, a field of corn for camouflage?
The frightened soldiers, just stalks themselves
in cultivated blue, dipped and hid, or so they thought—
their crouching image everywhere, like evening
through some giant harp. The corncobs burst
and rained about them, the brindled, bullet-blasted
leaves. On one dead man, the kernels' milk
had glued thick corn silk to his throat.
It swayed a bit in August wind, from
breastbone toward his shoulderline.
As I have seen some bloodless moss
sway from hothouse trees.

The Sitters

Mathew Brady

I. 1843

The clove at his gum line softens, seeps its sharp tea
to his tongue. He hums, troubles the stem
and sprocket head. He is walking down Beekman Street,
Samuel Morse to his left, on his right the damp road—
then two head-shaking jennets, the snap of their long ears
like gloved hands clapping.

On a rooftop above, Morse has fashioned
a glass cottage—a wall-cloak of spun nothingness—
to amplify light, to make from the camera's eye
less a stare than a blink. Long blink.
"It's a greenhouse for sitters," he says,
"their neck-stems steadied by a padded brace,
their faces abloom with the formerly hidden,
the intricate age lines just under our vision."

They sit both within and apart, the city
like a vine climbing each window.

II. JULY 17, 1861

He rides both within
and apart. Before him,

artillery caissons, supply wagons,
troops on foot, on horseback.
Behind him, the ribboned sleighs
of whorehouse madams,
flutists, lapdogs, four
Congressmen, their cart
of champagne and cold chicken.
And "What's that wagon?"
someone asks. "Black-shrouded
as a hearse, and making
with its passage a kind of
palpitation—like cattle
trotting a frozen lake."

Or bones? No: in dove-gray,
dust-proof cloaks, one hundred
glass plates flutter. Then
the icy clink of bromide bottles.
For days the slim parade
advances, although the wheels,
in grim illusion, spin
their gestures of retreat. From
Long Bridge, past the yellow woods,
to the wide plateau of

Centerville, one line,
then two:

the infantry
across the plain,
the brilliant watchers
higher still. And from
the ridge a preening woman
laughs into a mirror:

"We ape them more
with each layer of dust.
As they do us, with
every glitter of saber blade."

III. JULY 20, 1861

Picture a ridge, arced like a sickle moon.
At its rim, an audience of
carriages, leaf trees. And one bent man
in a linen duster, lost to a black-hooded camera.
And one thin road that drops, then
turns, then spills across a small plateau

where a sudden silence lingers.
There, in scrub and a bramble of dogwood dust,
one army waits as another
approaches. Friends perhaps? A man
with a chin-strap beard steps forward, waves. Then

the muskets start. The bearded man
and those behind him
turn, rush in panic up the thin road,
over stunted scrub and horsehair blankets,
carriages that buck, then tumble,
in the chopped wave of their bodies.
There are bullets like pox
in the milky oaks, in velvet lapels and picnic baskets.
Fallen, the bearded man sees to his left

the opal buttons of a woman's blouse. But no,
they are droplets of bile from a carriage horse.
And what is that shape turning toward him,
in the heat and summer wind? A man
bent over a steam gun?
Some ruffling bird, flapping
dark then light in the oak trees?
What is that flapping, like great wings? There

in the oak trees, is that
the human soul?

IV. 1896

"Could it be?" Someone speaks at the edge of his deathbed.
"A beam that can pass through flesh, Brady?
Can catch forever on a sea-green screen, our
innerness?" Then the voice disappears down a hallway.

He watches the snow fill his hospital window,
all the horse carts outside muffled. A beam?
To capture his heart in its flaccid canter?
His lungs that have thickened to leathered sacks?
High on a snow-wrapped sycamore branch

something plumed cracks a yellow beak,
spreads the fan of its dappled wing,
looks left, right—a sound like muffled hooves?—dips
its dappled head and preens.

SIX IN ALL

FOUR

The pulpit lilies gaped and dipped. The coffin's velvet
cast its nap in variative strips, as wind
might cast a summer's wheat. Asleep, they said,
she looks asleep—if sleep can suck the cheek skin down,
can still the lids to bone. I think

she had six words in all. And so she thought
in reds and whites, in hard-spun
roundnesses. One afternoon,
my father pressed her fingers to his pipe, breathed in,
exhaled, breathed in, that she might feel, like
some enchanted heart, the pipe bowl flare and ebb.
From that time on, she tracked its brier flutterings,

and all the spheres about her: the rigid arc
of radishes, the nurse's knees
that rose and sank beneath her white-knit stockings
like undersides of dying fish.

On the pane beside my sister's face,
the glass plate negative reveals a soldier
dead for weeks, or starved before his death,
his belly just a sunken sling between the bracket
of his hips. Above it all his snow-white belt

orbits like a jester's hoop. The hoop and then a gap
of air, and then the darkened bones of him. And

to the right, in sawgrass and a twining vetch,
his cup and round canteen.
"Death's thimbles" Father called the cups,
the way they steered to softer cloth
a bullet's leaded point. Invisibly the soldiers ran,
until the moonlight caught the cups, until
each pockmarked curve of tin
flared its dimpled bull's-eye.

And so we die of glimmer after all.

Jane's nurse was kind, but by her presence
verified the death at hand. We longed each night
to watch her lift her cape, drape its hood across
her hair, step into the field. The night absorbed her
instantly, the open, blue-black flapping cape
no more than tree limb, shrubbery. Departing,
she was just the world, the way the world
recedes at night. Then at the ridge
she turned to wave
and flashed her ghastly whiteness back at us.

The Suicide of
Clover Adams: 1885

All the bodies like fallen cattle.
And the snub-brimmed caps. The war. Civil.
Brady's shadow, at times, rinses a photograph
with its black pond. But the image I keep

is a blasted meadow. Burdock, bloated sacs
of lungwort. And up from the earth's fresh trough,
I think, the mineral scent of ripped grasses.

Henry slumps in the grip of a toothache.

If I were real, I would help him. But I
am the fabric of well-water—slick and transparent—
my voice a bird where my shoulder should be.

In the Doctrine of Signatures, each plant
cures the body it mimics.
So the liver-shaped leaves of hepatica
temper the liver's jaundice, and snuff
from the snapdragon's tapered neckline
heals the tubular body of the human throat.

Heart leaf and toothwort.

Steam from the kettle
has cast a late dew on the ladles.

And a privacy to each of the windows.
In print after print, Brady centered the men
facing east. The sandbags and cannons.
One midday, I centered our cousins with an eastward
glance, fresh for the incoming hour.
In the darkroom musk, they
rose through potassium baths
with the languorous ripples of flounders . . .

Steam. Its simmering mist.
If I were real, I would offer a flower. But I

have taken a body of water, stirred
through with cyanide salts. Slick and transparent,
they stroke their signature to the echoing self.
Which is nothing. And from which
nothing rises at all.

Edison: 1910

Dressed in an ebony suit,
could the soul of William James, they asked me, slip
past the bakery counter, his slack lapels
dusty with flour? Or walk on the cobbles
in those soft shoes? It was God, of course,
not James they questioned. And No, I said, No
suit, no Deity. We are the finite, meat-mechanisms

of matter. The uproar then! He was *seen*—brown shoes,
trousers—all the newsprint dripping with sightings!
Look down to your own shoes, I told them. There,
in the fluoroscope's green wash, your Inmost Essence

flexes. I remember Dally in his white coat,
week after week, bent
to the X-ray's beam, to the bloat
of ghostly photos, as the peephole burned its round tattoo
on his brow and cheekbone. How the beam itself
nibbled him—fingers, toes, hair, spleen.

A lantern through dust, he whispered, is a kind of gill.
It was Wednesday, a week from his death, some
childhood dust storm storming again.
He spoke of its wind and the launched soil,
the anemone-sway of the darkened sheep, as slowly,
they crossed, recrossed

the smallest arc of battered turf.
And lamplight in the barn,

although it was midday. And although it was midday
the sunset began. Crimson, he said,
just over the sheep, just over the alders, the yellow
sweep of hedgerow. And false, of course, some light
at play on the facets of dust. But . . . wonderful,

he told me. His bones on the fluoroscope's pale screen
tapered and flared, the nodules of toe-tips
black, protrusive, like ghastly buds—a presence

that walks with us always, I think, flexing its grip
invisibly. And that visible sunset he fashioned,
slumped on its false horizon?
Some vibrant, wind-churned absence,
defined by dust and reverence.

Muybridge

These are the names of the horses:
Occident. Elaine. Abe Edgerton. Clay.
With a shutter's quick clickings, I stopped them,
then dealt the divine and its opposite, picture
by square picture: the unwinged body in flight—
two hooves pushing off, then one, then none—
and the pact of that flight: groping forelegs,
the groping, horn-sheathed toes.

Time after time, from the beauty of motion
came the pickets of stasis! And yet,

I remember the heart of a snapping turtle,
grotesque in its florid two-step. We had peeled back
the breastplate, dragged the body by cart past the eyes
of twelve cameras, the cart wheels tripping the shutters.
I could not watch the motion then, but
turned instead to the open mouth, the palate ridged
like a walnut shell, turned instead to the static photos—
where something, hollow and weightless, a poppy perhaps,
where something twelve times, like a poppy,
was pressed and released by a rhythmic wind.

I stopped the pine snake and horse. Or better,
I held them. Field cat. Hawk. The wake
of a coastline steamer.

In a northwest harbor one autumn, I watched a meadow
flood to a cranberry pond. Then a man with a rake
pulled the blunt berries from their soft vines.
They floated around him, filling the surface,
red and amber and that last yellow before it is red.
He stood in the pond, and the berries, like evening,
absorbed him, his boots and thighs. They covered each
glisten of the water, until only the sharpest shining
survived, where the rake cut a path through the redness.

What would I hold? All. Almost all. The poppy
in its soft backdrop. The hawk. And the horse,
the great weight on the last hoof,
then the lifting of that weight.
What would I stop? Only the path
of the rake, I think, that arc
reaching over the pond and the circling hour.
Only the need to reach over.

The Breaking-Aways

Samuel F. B. Morse

The wire was bare, a horse-flank sheen,
and I wrapped it, yard by laborious yard,
in cotton—and once for the Hudson River, in tar-black
and pitch. Great coils with the lime scent of
solder. And peopling my rooms:
magnets and pendulums, coupling, repelling,
like the long married.

"What hath God wrought!" I tapped, dashes and dots
ticking toward Baltimore. Greetings. Stop.
Regret. Stop. And the sound? Like hail
through an April elm.

Often, I think of our lives
as distinctions, quick
breaking-aways. From some vast, celestial streaming
we are particles. The splendid particulars.

When I was a boy,
I followed the musk of a creek bed
out through the forest. Just sludge
and cabbage bloat. Then a woman's scream,
far off to my left, long and unwavering—

～

but no, a field cat on a flat stone—but no,
larger, thick as a dog.
I remember elms, the paste of the creek bed.
How I covered my ears with their cold lobes
to soften the screaming. And just before
backing away, released the lobes, then pressed again,
then again—and made from that
scream, from that wondrous outrush,
something apart from wonder.

Lawrence and Edison
in New Jersey: 1923

"Like a plum!" Lawrence says. "Frieda in anger
is a burst plum. Taut skin, the mouth's lolling gash.
Her face. And the simpering rains of Mexico."
But Edison, deaf, hears "heckles so," and "Isn't that true,"
he replies, "the public, the heckling swarms."

They are walking past blossoms of lupine and aster,
the aquatic stray of a weathered stump.
It is sunset, their shadows edemic
on the pathway before them. "That stump,"
Lawrence says, "its snout-crust of barnacle lichen
holds the backward grin of the blue whale."

"Yes, the platinum spin of the fuel," sings the elder—
"the current's coil—then a carbon thread
glowing for hours." And so they continue, man
of the flesh, man of the mind: luster and circuit,
ripple and system. Past cattle, grain troughs,

then out toward a withered pond, Lawrence bobbing
near Edison's ear, its unwavering tangent of lobe crease.
At the water's frayed edge, they sit, Lawrence
lost to the ponds of his childhood—black mouths
in the fields like mineworks—Edison courting
the consummate marriage—motion and sound—

That the cantering profile of Muybridge's dobbin, he thinks,
might snortle and whinny! He smiles, leisurely
stabs at his dead ear. *Phono. Graph.* A little wax
gleams in the whorls of his thumb tip.
The head in deafness is a black pond, some occasional
wash-strokes of fin. He straightens, then:

"You might talk on my knee with the Morse code."
But Lawrence, distracted, hears "harsh cold"
and quickly the pond gels, the bodies of skaters stroke
in unison, as their scarves in unison
lift with their scarf-shaped breath. "We would circle
together as one," Lawrence says. "Round and around."

"Yes, round and around it spins, the disc
with its captured world. And the stylus—Lawrence!—
it glides on the wax like a blade."

SIX IN ALL

FIVE

Along the foreground's dusty scrub, a cello's ice-white shadow
slinked toward my mother's hem. Beyond the frame,
the army band was mute across the ground: one flute,
then thwirrs of shuffling cards, like pigeon wings.

And to the left the birds themselves,
the homing cotes and landing boards.

My parents posed against an oak, Jane's carriage thick
beside them—no Jane at all, except for fists
that groped above the basket rim like pearly mums.
My mother smiled, leaned back across my father's arm.
A soldier coughed. No war in sight, no long descent
from dampened bone, to human grain, to
just some frontal profile in the earth. And so,

when from the trees the little shape began,
arced toward us like a triggered stone, we held
our leisure. The bird stroked down, the burl of message
on its leg just words—although I think their secret
finished us. In time, hawk-ripped or ripped by shot,

still the pigeons stuttered back. I wondered
at their steadfastness. The jerking head, the shad-roe eye—
they seemed to crack through clouds

like energy and nothing more. Not drawn by words, of course,
but . . . what? The mate? The suet bead? The humid cote
or human hand? The chime of some vestigial song?
I cannot find the words for this. I think

of oaks, a shutter's gape, the field drums
curved like calves across the ground.

Burning the Fields

1.

In the windless late sunlight of August,
my father set fire to a globe of twine. At his back,
the harvested acres of bluegrass and timothy
rippled. I watched from a shallow hill
as the globe, chained to the flank of his pickup truck,
galloped and bucked down a yellow row, arced
at the fire trench, circled back,
arced again, the flames behind
sketching first a *C,* then closing to *O*—a word
or wreath, a flapping, slack-based heart,

gradually filling. To me at least. To the mare
beside me, my father dragged a gleaming fence,
some cinch-corral she might have known,
the way the walls moved rhythmically,
in and in. And to the crows, manic
on the thermals? A crescent of their planet,

gone to sudden sun. I watched one stutter
past the fence line, then settle
on a Hereford's tufted nape,
as if to peck some safer grain, as if

the red-cast back it rode
contained no transformations.

2.

A seepage, then, from the fire's edge: there
and there, the russet flood of rabbits.
Over the sounds of burning, their haunted calls
began, shrill and wavering, as if
their dormant voice strings
had tightened into threads of glass.

In an instant they were gone—the rabbits,
their voices—over the fire trench,
into the fallows. My father walked
near the burn line, waved up to me, and from
that wave, or the rippled film of heat,

I remembered our porch in an August wind,
how he stepped through the weathered doorway,
his hand outstretched with some
book-pressed flower, orchid or lily, withered
to a parchment brown. *Here,* he said, but
as he spoke it atomized before us—

pulp and stem, the pollened tongue,
dreadful in the dancing air.

3.

Scummed and boxcar thin,
six glass-walled houses stretched beside our fields.
Inside them, lilies, lilies—

a thousand shades of white, I think.
Eggshell, oyster, parchment, flax.

Far down the black-mulched beds, they seemed
ancestral to me, the fluted heads of
dowagers, their meaty, groping,
silent tongues. They seemed
to form perspective's chain:
cinder, bone, divinity . . .

4.

My father waved. The crows set down.
By evening, our fields took the texture
of freshened clay, a sleek

and water-bloated sheen, although no water
rested there—just heat and ash
united in a slick mirage. I crossed the fence line,
circled closer, the grasses all around me
collapsing into tufts of smoke. Then as I bent
I saw the shapes, rows and rows of tougher stems—

brittle, black, metallic wisps, like something grown
to echo grass. The soot was warm,
the sky held smoke in a jaundiced wing,
and as a breeze crossed slowly through,
stems glowed—then ebbed—
consecutively. And so revealed a kind of path,
and then a kind of journey.

The Weathervanes

Polished by offshore, sand-pocked winds,
they leered up from a backdrop of bay: swordfish
and salmon, the whale, its tin ball of spume.
Up the hill toward the meadows,
each flickered its household's obsession:
the fisherman's cod, the dairyman's guernsey,
the goose perched high on the quilt maker's shakes.
And the sloop, the trembling canoe, the rooster,
sheep, all taut on their off-center spindles, all turned

from the bay. In my attic room I watched them,
and my neighbor's metal silhouette—horse
and carriage, driver, whip, two tiny reins
like filaments. It gleamed with a copper urgency:
ears back, mane back, the horse in perpetual gasp,
in the swimmer's perpetual reach and stroke,
the man stiff-set from speed and longing,
from that tremor just over the human heart.
And down the steep hill from their carriage,

the static parade of fins and wings.
Sometimes an on-shore wind would flip them,
all in one motion, back toward the sea.
Sometimes I would look to my neighbor's window,
past the pond with its living gabble of geese,
through the russet-cast hush of his parlor.

He held his cello as a sheepshearer would,
knees clamped on the body, left hand crossing
a fret of ribs, bearing down at last
on the pressure point, just over the darkened heart.
He would stop in the utter stillness a moment,
shape over shadow. Then his right arm
stretched to its see-saw journey.
And then the thrumming song.

Safe

Safe, we thought.
The flood waters nestled
the arc of their udders, but no higher,
dewlaps, flanks, even the tips of the briskets,
dry. All day they stood
in the seascape meadow,
their square heads turned from the wind.
By evening they were dead.
Chill, we learned, not drowning,
killed them—the milk vein
thick on the floor of the chest
filling with cold, stunning the heart.
We had entered the house, where silt water
sketched on the walls and doorways
a single age-ring. When we looked back
they had fallen, only the crests of their bodies
breaking the waterline. I remember
the wind and a passive light,
then the jabber of black grackles
riding each shoulder's upturned blade.

Depth of Field

Specula. Gauze in a halo of disinfectant.
We sit in the small room, dimmed
by the x-ray of my father's chest
and the screen's anemic light. Because on film
the spots are dark, my mother asks
if, in the lung, they might be white: some
hopeless sense of the benign. My father smiles.
Outside the window, a winter storm
continues. Across the park, the bronze-cast generals
spur their anguished horses, each posture
fierce with rearing. Nostrils, lips, the lidless eyes.
Now all the flung-back heads have filled with snow.

The Fan

Not birds or vines, not full-blown roses
trellised through its wooden ribs,
but *story:* sunset, farm, eight children husking corn.
And as my father dies, draped
on the respirator's rhythmic wheeze,
I bend to fan him,

offer a more natural wind.
His eyelids do not meet completely
and I create within those slender gaps
a world of seeing, imagine he can look beyond
the sheets and tubing, beyond the skin-thin, painted wing
that strokes and slowly strokes,

and down its roadway arcing toward the farm.
A house, spar left. Spar right, a barn.
And in between, eight children
on a sediment of curling husks. Five
crouch and peel—a sound like ripping gauze—one
flings from the pitchfork's triple tines
a plume of leaves and corn silk. Dead-center,

two stand and wrestle. Arms straight,
hands clamped on opposing shoulders, they lean
with their chests, pull back with their hips,

and frame with their standoff bodies
a perfect circle of sunlit road.

He does not sleep. Or always sleeps,
two rims of lightless iris
blind to the visible hours. I fold the fan
and the house closes into itself, the barn closes,
down and down. And the children pull in their arms,
slip back through the slender rooms, the slender,
straw-filled stalls, until only the two remain,

locked in their static circle. And if they could move—
pull and repel—their rhythm
might reflect a kind of breathing. But
they are caught, of course, halted by the tension
of both drawing in and letting go,
and so the circle their bodies make
reflects a kind of breathlessness.

After-Image

Three weeks past my father's death
his surgeons, in pond-green smocks, linger,
trail after me from dream to porch, down
the bark and needle pathway toward the river.
One nudges me, explains as he did weeks ago
the eye's propensity for opposites, why green
displaced their bleached-white coats. "Looking up
from the tablet of a patient's blood," he says,
"the red-filled retina will cast a green
on every white it crosses." A phantom wash
on a neighboring sleeve. "It startles us,"
he tells me. And: "Green absorbs the ghosting."
                    Then he is gone, the path
returning to boot brush and the squirrel ratchets
my father loved. It is noon, the sky
through the tree limbs a sunless white.
I've come to watch the spawning salmon
stalled in the shallow pools. Age
has burned them a smoky red, though
their heads are silver, like helmets. Just over
the mossy floor, they float unsupported,
or supported by air their gills have winnowed.
I think I will gather them soon, deep
in the eye, red and red and red,
then turn to the canopy of sky and cedars.
It will support them soon, the green.

SIX IN ALL

SIX

Behind my back, before my family, the elms
have flared, dropped leaves, regathered them in tiny buds.
Before me, behind my family, the limes are still,
drawn out through shades of darkening
by nothing more than light. Last night

I read a tracker's lore, half truth, I think,
half wonderment—how, fleeing, one man mounted stilts,
another fastened to his soles the stiffened gnarls
of cows' hooves. Such fussings over twists
in dust! But beauty, too, that one can read
a residue, that from the profile of a stride
a body might be crafted.

We're faded now, my mother's sleeve, my sister's spidered
fists. For someone standing next to me,
we're only hatchings on the glass, like

hairline prints the heron leaves,
its tracks across the sandy bank first shallow—here—
then deeper as a fish was snared, then deeper still
as, taking flight, it most was wedded to the ground.

But I've described a positive, the darkened prints
across the glass. In fact these hatch-lined negatives
echo what was pale in us. And if the bird had truly walked

in tandem with my family's path, its tracks
would yield a vacancy, like whitened lashes
of the dead. In this inert, inverted world,
what most engaged the passing light tumbled first
to nothingness. My father lifts a brier pipe,
a soot-black bulb reversed to ice.
The stem, the bowl, the mouthpiece gone.
It is his smoke that lingers.